REACHING OUT

Robert S. Welch

REACHING OUT
Lessons of God

TATE PUBLISHING *& Enterprises*

Reaching Out
Copyright © 2010 by Robert S. Welch. All rights reserved.

No part of this publication may be reproduced, stored in a retrieval system or transmitted in any way by any means, electronic, mechanical, photocopy, recording or otherwise without the prior permission of the author except as provided by USA copyright law.

The opinions expressed by the author are not necessarily those of Tate Publishing, LLC.

Published by Tate Publishing & Enterprises, LLC
127 E. Trade Center Terrace | Mustang, Oklahoma 73064 USA
1.888.361.9473 | www.tatepublishing.com

Tate Publishing is committed to excellence in the publishing industry. The company reflects the philosophy established by the founders, based on Psalm 68:11,
"The Lord gave the word and great was the company of those who published it."

Book design copyright © 2010 by Tate Publishing, LLC. All rights reserved.
Cover design by Kandi Evans
Interior design by Lindsay B. Behrens

Published in the United States of America

ISBN: 978-1-61566-808-3
1. Religion / Mysticism   2. Religion / Christian Life / Inspirational
09.12.21

DEDICATIONS

I am dedicating this book to God. The one who truly knows every fiber of my being. I have always known of him but he has shown me how to truly know him. He has shown me a peace through love that I did not think was possible. He has brought me into the light, and that is where I will remain forever.

ACKNOWLEDGMENTS

Maureen my wife, my true love, and my best friend who has always been there for me on this incredible ride of faith, we ride together.

My son Rob, the first miracle in my life.

Mom, who has shown me how to have faith by living it.

Bob and Helene, thank you for opening my eyes so I could find my path. I am blessed to have you in my life.

Linda, for giving me the opportunity and the knowledge to be a great Farrier. You have changed my life forever.

Sharon, without any hesitation you made my last hurdle disappear. You took away my worries and replaced them with joy

Thank you to everyone who helped make this book a reality. You know who you are! May you be in God's light forever.

TABLE OF CONTENTS

Foreword 11
Introduction 13
Removing My Blinders 17
Following His lead. 29
Tank 37
Never Ending Love 41
Never alone 51
God Watches Over Us All 53
Forgiveness 59
Roses for Maryanne 63
Sending Us Peace 67
The Week of Marys 71
Dinner guests 81
Hootie 85
God's conduit 89

Signs All Around Us	97
God's Toy Box	107
Angels among us	111
No Boundaries	119
Love again	125
Celebrate life	127
Showing Faith	131
Reincarnation	135
Divine timing	139
Grandmother's love	143
Epilogue	147

FOREWORD

Spiritual lights would be a good description of Rob and his wife, Maureen. Some people may possibly see them as private and reclusive, but they have been able to open up their minds and hearts to the presence of God. Rob's willingness to pursue God's purpose for him in this life is an example for all of us. Through this acceptance, he has helped many people come to terms with grief, loss, and tragedy; helping to move them forward to health and contentment. Read on, dear readers; open your thoughts and mind to the spiritual beings that Rob encounters. Know that you too can be helped through life by their loving presence. They make themselves available to bring us peace, love, joy, and understanding. Stay calm and focused on spirit. Let these readings affirm to you that you are not walking this earth alone. Your loved ones that have passed are with you to comfort and guide you. Start today with even a small amount of trust in God's love for you and you will see your life change. Know that Rob's readings are true and that Rob is fulfilling God's purpose for him in this life.

May you be blessed so you can also fulfill yours.

In Peace,

Cynthia L. Valente

INTRODUCTION

This is a book of reaching out to God and how he reached back to me. He has led me down a path that I did not think was possible. I have been passing along messages and have been following the breadcrumbs that God has laid out for me for many years. I am honored to be able to share it with everyone who reads it. One of my messages from God was that I was to write a series of books on how he has brought me to where I am now.

My first big sign that things did not happen by accident, that there are no coincidences, was my sixteenth birthday. Maureen and I had been dating for almost a year. My Mom was kidding around with me about sweet sixteen and "never been kissed." I noticed that Maureen was blushing.

I thought that she was just embarrassed about the subject. When my mom left the room, Maureen asked me why my mom was giving her a hard time. I laughed because my mom was talking to me, not Mo. I asked Maureen when her birthday was. It was the day after mine. We laughed, because I was one day older than her. When my mom returned, we told her and she asked who Maureen's doctor was. We had the same doctor, same hospital, probably the same nursery. All three of us were surprised.

We married at the age of nineteen and had a beautiful baby boy. We always knew that everything happened for a reason. We had faith in God, and knew that some day everything would make sense.

When I was in my early teens, I used to turn up music very loud to drown out all the thoughts that seemed to bombard me. I always felt like I was being chased by something. I would stare at the horizon like something or someone was calling to me.

As I got older, I really thought I was losing it. When I would talk to someone, my mind would wander, thinking of things that had nothing to do with the conversation we were having. I believed that when I got older, Maureen would have a difficult time keeping me here; that I would slip away mentally. It wasn't until I met the *"animal communicator"* and her husband that things made sense. They opened my eyes forever.

REMOVING MY BLINDERS

The stories I am writing are about God and the wonderful and amazing journey he has given me. These stories are about faith and about believing. I have to admit that I am still amazed at how God's timing, humor, love, and understanding are so incredible. It is very humbling. For some reason, he chose me for this gift. For this I am so very grateful. I believe it's partially because I am not afraid to speak up and tell people their message, no matter how wild it might seem to me. It always seems to make sense to them. I guess it's like reading someone else's mail; it's not supposed to make sense to me.

God reaches out to all of us, whether we believe in him or not; no matter what religion or beliefs we have. All you have to do is listen. God doesn't yell, he whispers. And if he does yell, it would be a good idea to listen. "Don't take that turn!" Or "Did I turn off the iron?" Chances are that the strong feeling or thought you had are right on. I have found that God uses everything and anything to get our attention, to get his message across, and to just let us know he is here. I have personally seen him use animals, flowers, newspapers, letters, loved ones who have passed ... the list goes on and on.

These stories are just that; messages of love, pure love, the kind of love that most people think is no longer here. When, in fact, it is all around you, surrounding you. All you have to do is take the time to let it in. Some people think messages and messengers are only in the Bible. God is here and now, and he still sends messages, and he still has his messengers to deliver them.

When God requested that I write this book to reach out and touch the masses, my first thought was *Do I really want to change my life that much?* I cherish my privacy and my peace and quiet; but

God has never led me astray. He asks for just one step, that's all. I take that one step and I always find a *breadcrumb*, something I was looking for or needed: confirmation that I am on the right path.

When I accepted that I was to write this book, all of a sudden people near and far started to suggest to me that I should write a book, just out of the blue. There was my breadcrumb. The truth is that I don't know where this will take me, but even if my message only reaches ten people, if it helps them, then I've done my job.

One night I received another breadcrumb. Mo and I were watching a movie when one of our dogs chased something across the floor into the corner. I got up and went over to see what it was. It was a tarantula; not what I had expected. I can safely say I have never had a tarantula in the house before. I knew that the tarantula was a sign from God; he was trying to get my attention. I also knew I should not wait on this one. It actually ran right in front of me. We know that there are tarantulas around. After all, we do live in the high desert where they live. But we certainly do not expect them in the house.

An animal sign to me is when an animal that is totally out of place enters your life either by running, flying, crawling or whatever it is that catches your attention. It is like they are yelling, "Hey look at me."

In the past I would refer to different books about how animal signs meant things spiritually. Each animal carried some kind of message to the person it was intended for. Then I would see how accurate they were by applying it to the situation. Well this one hit the nail right on the head. The sign that the tarantula carried was about moving forward with writing this book.

That tarantula really got my attention, bringing my message to the surface. It was a turning point for me.

Up until this point I was trying to avoid the answer to the question that I asked God, which was, "What next, what do you want me to do next?" I then realized that there really was only one answer: to follow God's lead. That is all there is.

After that sign there was no doubt what I needed to do. I knew that I had to get started on God's book right away. When I give someone a message, I call it a "reading." This book is a record of some of these "readings." I changed people's first names for privacy, and I sometimes leave out parts of the reading that I feel I am not supposed to write about.

What I consider the beginning of my spiritual journey is when I learned how to shoe horses. I started learning how to shoe horses when I was thirty-two years old. My wife Mo (short for Maureen), thought it would be a good idea, as we had horses. Our farrier was a woman named Jean, and she taught me how to shoe. One day, she was telling Mo and me that she had a customer who could talk to animals. I laughed because I did not think that I would ever meet a real communicator, even though I did believe that there had to be someone out there somewhere who could do this.

One day Mo and I went out to feed our horses and we discovered that Tigger and Jackpot were missing. We checked the pasture and found the electric fence was pulled into the pasture, and we found the tracks of a large dog that had chased them around until they went through the fence, jumped an irrigation ditch, and ran down a dirt road behind the pasture. We found them down the road, uninjured, and brought them home. My older gelding, Shasta, was standing in his stall and would not go into the pasture on his own. I thought this was the perfect opportunity to put the "horse whisperer" to the test. Mo brought three of our horses, Tigger, Jackpot and Shasta to Jean's where she had an appointment with Fran, the animal communicator.

Fran tried to talk to Jackpot and Tigger, but they were very apprehensive about it. So she went to Shasta, who proceeded to tell her all about the dog and how it chased Jackpot and Tigger; how they jumped the ditch, and ran down the road. Shasta told her he knew he would be safe in his stall, because it was close to the house, which is where we found him that morning. Well, let me tell you … Wow! That was not what I had expected. I was thinking more along the lines of "*My grass is green, my water is wet, and the sky is blue.*" Mo was so impressed that she asked Fran if she had ever taught anyone how to talk to animals. Fran told her yes, as a matter-of-fact, she had a class every other Wednesday evening, and Maureen was more than welcome to come.

Mo started going to those classes at the time in my life when I was working evenings and not able to attend. She went to a few classes and told me that the people who taught it were very spiritual and did everything through God and Jesus. Mo went to a few meetings and stopped because she started to get strange feelings like something was not right.

Mo had missed the first class where they talked about protecting yourself against bad energies. Bad energies bring chaos into your life like bad dreams, strange feelings, and frustration. God puts this "red flag warning system" in all of us. It's when something happens and you immediately get that alert of something is not right. The "protection" part is about saying a prayer and asking only for messages from God and Heaven. It's like your wearing a cloak and when you open it is when you expose your soul. God gives you free will and it's up to you who you want to get your messages from good or bad.

I changed to the day shift. Mo asked me if I was interested in going with her to the meetings again and I agreed to go. I was happy to see that the classes always started off with a prayer to God and Jesus, and they were based around God and love. I was very drawn in by what they had to say, it was like I had been waiting my whole life to hear this. Fran and her husband Mel spoke about all of God's creatures, and how the way you speak to animals is the same way you hear God and his angels. I was amazed. I could not get enough. I had always believed in God and that everything happens for a reason.

I started to see auras about a month after my first meeting with Fran and Mel. They taught me how to quiet my thoughts and how to just watch and listen. I began to feel like God had a message for me. Like he was trying to say something, but I just could not understand him. My left ear would ring whenever I got this feeling.

Fran and Mel would encourage me to read spiritual books to help me learn more. They would loan me books that would sit on my table and collect dust. I would pick them up, but after a few paragraphs I would loose interest. I felt like the books were not for me. A few months later I was praying and I asked Jesus why I could not get anything from the books that I had borrowed. He told me it was because if I had read them they would be my first impression. Jesus said that he wanted *his* messages to be the first thing that came to me. Mo and I went to Fran and Mel's classes for several months until we felt like it was time to move on.

My first message was on Christmas morning. He said he was, "Malachi, from the Golden White Light." This is how he introduced himself to me. I had no idea who he was (until later that day, when my son said he was in the Bible), but he said he was from heaven, so I asked him to continue. He wanted me to bring a message to a detective working on a year-old missing child case. I can't share the details, because the case is still open, but I was thinking, "Wow, I know things about this case that weren't released to the public. What if they think I had something to do with it?" But whenever I felt that way, I would get a feeling of peacefulness, and I would think, "Why would God let me be hurt for passing on a message for him?"

Looking back now, I realize that the message that I had passed on was just a part of many things, like spokes in a wheel. One part was to let the detectives know that God is on their side and to have more faith in the people. My spoke of the wheel had to do with faith; faith in myself and most of all, faith in God. He really does see everything. Nothing is an accident. We may not understand it now, but someday we will.

With my first message I decided one thing. I was not to charge for the readings (I never received a message to charge for the readings). I feel it would not be right to charge for a gift that God has given to me.

FOLLOWING HIS LEAD

I started feeling like God had a bigger purpose for me; like he was asking me to do something for him. This went on and on for several weeks. At the same time, I started to get visions of myself performing a healing on Jean, our farrier. Jean had breathing problems similar to asthma; she carried an inhaler with her all the time. In my vision, I had my left hand on her left shoulder and my right hand was moving, palm up, going up her back. I kept making believe I didn't see the vision (like God wouldn't know!), and I hoped it would stop. I wasn't a very touch-feely kind of person at the time, but after several weeks, I started to feel like doing the healing on Jean was more serious.

Around the same time, I got a vision of myself putting shoes on a horse. This concerned me, because I was making good money where I worked, with full benefits and three weeks vacation time. I was working fifty to sixty hours a week. Where was I going to get my clientele if I started shoeing? Well, my last vision of healing Jean was God telling me that if I did not do this healing, she would be carrying an oxygen bottle within six months. Jean already carried an inhaler (because of her breathing). So I got on the phone immediately and told her of my vision and my message. To my surprise, she wanted to know when I wanted to do this. I told her tomorrow. Jean and her husband Jim came over.

I still remember the day, a Tuesday. I was told by God to tell her to picture a ray of golden white light coming from heaven onto her forehead, going through her body, and coming out through the up-turned palms of her hands. Then I closed my eyes and prayed to God, *"Please show me how and what you want me to do to heal Jean."* Again I saw my left hand on her left shoulder and my right hand on her lower back.

I saw a ray of golden white light coming down from heaven into my head. I could feel it going through me like a warm, energetic sensation. I started to run my right hand up her back; it looked like I was scooping whipped cream out of her lungs. Jean started to cough a little and I continued this for five to ten minutes. When we were done, I watched Jean take a deep breath without any of the congestion she had before we started. I was surprised and unsure if it was all in her head or not. Jean sat down on the couch and said she felt very tired. I asked her if it was from what I had just done, and she replied that it was not; that she was working too hard. She said she had too many horses to shoe and she was planning on letting about half of her customers go.

That was when I knew something was definitely going on. After my vision of shoeing horses, I asked God how I was going to make a living. But here it was, I had done the healing he had wanted me to do, and I was delivered a career. What I didn't understand then was that this was how God was going to make me mobile, so he could get me to those people who needed to receive their message. When I first started getting messages for people, I was a little shy about telling them; I didn't want people to think I was weird.

I still don't want people to think I'm weird, but now I look at it this way: when I pass on to heaven and am standing at the Pearly Gates, the only opinion about how I lived my life that's going to matter is God's. He is the only one who knows if I've done everything and said everything he wanted me to say. This is why I am writing this book.

Another one of the first messages I received was for Jean. At that time in my life, I was a farrier traveling around practicing my new gift, which was communicating with animals. It was a great proving ground. The best way to practice communicating is with animals you don't know anything about; then ask the owners if the things the animals said made sense to them.

I saw a vision of Jean pulling the hind shoes off of a horse. I could see the color of the horse from the hips back. It was bay (brown). She used to kneel down on one knee and put the horse's hind foot on her other knee because it was easier on the horse to hold their hoof lower to the ground (though also more hazardous for the farrier). Then the vision stopped and I heard Elvis singing "*Blue Christmas.*" I called and told her of my vision and I asked her to be careful, because the vision was of great pain and sorrow. She later called me back after shoeing a horse she thought might have been the horse she needed to watch for, but I still had the feeling of danger.

The following week, she called me again and told me about a horse she had shod that day. The horse immediately had her attention, and after talking to the owners about his issues, she figured this was the one. He was a paint horse, bay and white, and from the hips back he was bay. One thing I admire about Jean is that she didn't freak out. She took the warning as just what it was supposed to be: Proceed with caution. As she was shoeing, the horse kicked at her before she was able to get the shoe off with the tool still attached to it. The tool that is used, called *"pullers,"* is shaped like pliers with twelve inch long handles. If she had been kneeling as she usually did, the tool would have punctured her in the back. When she told me this, I no longer had the feeling of danger for her.

One night, Jean called after we had gone to bed and left us a message asking for us to send some prayers for her sister's grandson Johnnie. He was sick and in the hospital. We were half–asleep and I really didn't think about the message until I woke up in the morning, and all I could think about was this little boy. I started praying to Jesus, "Please heal him," the same prayer, over and over and over. All of a sudden, I was shown a vision of a little boy facing me. He was suspended in the dark with his arms and legs spread. I kept praying, and as I prayed for him, his lungs and chest began to glow with a golden light, rays shining outward. It was beautiful. I could hear Tim McGraw singing his song "Everywhere," with the lyrics "See you in Albuquerque" repeatedly over and over. I had a feeling that I was finished; that God was telling me I had done all I could, it was in his hands now.

At that time I was working part time nights and shoeing horses during the day; Mo called me in tears to tell me that the baby we had been praying for had been diagnosed with a lung condition (R.S.V.), but when the doctors came in to check on him that morning, he was fine. They figured that they must have misdiagnosed him and they released him that morning. He lives with his family in Albuquerque, New Mexico. I did get to meet Johnnie six months later. It was very interesting. When I walked into the room, he stared into my eyes like he knew me. It was a very touching moment. I really loved the way he looked at me; I'll never forget that look. It was that, "Don't I know you from somewhere" look.

I learned in praying for Johnnie that prayers really do work. I found it very interesting that Johnnie recognized me.

TANK

I have a friend named Chris, who I had a spiritual discussion with one Friday, about how I communicated with both angels and animals, and how it was about listening. She said she believed, but her husband was not so open. She kept telling him to stop giggling. I told her it was alright, I understood it was strange to hear someone openly talk about hearing messages from angels and the voices of animals.

The following Monday, we got a call from Chris. Her horse Reo had been struggling with colic (a digestive problem or intestinal blockage which can be deadly) all morning. She had taken her to the vet, who had put a scope down Reo's throat and found that the horse had a twisted intestine, which surgery could not fix. There was nothing Chris could do but bring Reo home and make her comfortable, and the vet would be out later in the day to put her to sleep before she was in too much pain.

We immediately went to see Reo. She was lying on the ground, bunched up like someone had kicked her in the gut. Chris was sitting on the ground cradling Reo's head in her lap while she cried. It was very upsetting to see Reo in such pain and to see Chris so upset about not being able to help her. I could see how much Chris loved Reo. When Chris looked up at us with her tear-filled eyes, she had that "Please help me," expression on her face. I had to take a deep breath, because I did not want to be overwhelmed with emotions. I wanted to keep my mind open for guidance from God and ask exactly what he wanted us to do. We told her we would pray for Reo and ask God for guidance.

God showed me to stand Reo up, which took some coaxing. When we had her standing, Mo and

I put our hands on her and prayed for guidance. When I prayed to take her pain away, I got visions of where to place my hands, and Mo did the same on the opposite side. This went on for an hour and a half to two hours. Then I got the message that we had done all we could, she was in God's hands now. Reo was walking better, but still looked concerned and uncomfortable. We put her back in her stall and told Chris to pray and to picture a golden white light surrounding Reo's abdomen. We also told Chris to picture Reo's intestine looking like two sausages, and then untwist the two sausages, and to picture this in the golden white light from heaven, and to continue praying through the night. We then told her it was in God's hands, that we had done all that we could.

While Chris, her husband Tom, and Mo were sitting with Reo, I felt something drawing me over to Tom's horse, Flop. I walked over to Flop and started to "talk to him" (telepathically). I asked Flop how he liked living here. He told me he really liked it. He liked it when Tom gave him affection and love, which he had not gotten where he lived before. Flop then told me that he liked it when Tom called him Tank. When Flop said this, he sent me a feeling of that *stick–your–chest–out–proud* feeling. I smiled, because I also got that feeling of, *"Here's your proof that I am communicating with Flop."* I went back and told Tom what Flop had said. Tom rolled his eyes and giggled, until I told him that Flop especially liked it when Tom called him, "Tank." Tom almost fell off his chair. He had never told anyone his nickname for Flop. We all had a good laugh.

The next morning, Chris called us with the good news. Chris asked if we knew of anyone who would be interested in cleaning Reo's stall, because she had obviously untwisted her intestine from the amount of poop that was in her stall. Reo was fine, with no signs of pain. The vet also called that morning, and the next, to check on Reo and be sure she was okay. They were very surprised to hear that she was fine. They said it was a miracle that she was okay.

NEVER ENDING LOVE

I had a customer, Ned, who was a rancher from Nebraska. He had been welding galvanized steel, which gave off dangerous gasses. About ten years earlier, these gasses gave him several strokes that left him in a wheel chair. He could still use his right arm pretty good. I met him through his daughter–in–law, Sharon, whose horses I shod. One day, when I was at their home shoeing her horse, God told me to tell her about my gift, communicating with animals. This was a few months after I first discovered I had a gift and was not sure who to talk to about it with. My message went something like this.

God: Tell her about your gift!
Me: Right now?
God: Yes!
Me: You mean right now?
God: Yes, right now!
Me: You mean like, right now?
God: Yes!

So you can see he is persistent, so I told her.

It scared her at first; I'm sure because no one had spoken to her about talking to horses before. So I talked to her stallion, who told me how he really enjoyed it when she sang *"My Darling Clementine"* to him. That definitely got her attention; she turned bright red. She was shocked; it was the song she sang to him all the time. There was her proof that I was the real thing.

One day, she came to me and asked Maureen and I to please come to the hospital to visit her mother–in–law, Bess (Ned's wife). Bess was in a coma and the doctors didn't quite know why. Sharon said that the room Bess was in was quite warm, and the hospital staff said that the air conditioning unit was fine. They could not explain why the room was so warm. Sharon felt that maybe the heat in the room was from *"bad things."* I told her that when a lot of angels are around sometimes it can get quite warm.

When Sharon asked if we could go visit, we went that day. It was quite warm in her room and she appeared to be resting peacefully in bed. I walked over to Bess's left side, Sharon was at her right side, and Maureen was at the foot of her bed. I started sending messages. I had never tried to communicate with anyone in a coma before. I asked if we could do anything to make her comfortable. She sent back, "Yes, I would like my face wiped with a moist facecloth." Before I could do this, Sharon was already going to get one. This showed me that other people do hear messages, but just don't recognize the difference between their thoughts and the message being sent to them. After that, we began to pray for Bess and trying to communicate with her through thought.

Bess started sending me messages to tell her husband that she would wait for him in heaven, so they could swing–dance like they used to. She showed me an image of her in a blue dress and described the dance hall they used to go to. I related this to Sharon to tell Ned, who was at home. Maureen was also communicating with her and asked why she didn't wake up. She told Maureen that she didn't know how to. Maureen put her hands on Bess's feet, Sharon put her hands on her right side, and I did the same on her left side. Maureen told Bess to picture herself in God's golden white light and to ask God for strength.

About two minutes after we started praying, Bess sat straight up in bed, opened her eyes, and looked around the room as though she had just woken up from a deep sleep. She didn't say anything, but she lay back down and relaxed back in the bed. Talk about a shocker, I didn't see that one coming! My mind was racing trying to take this all in. When we left the hospital I felt that we had done everything that we were supposed to do spiritually for Bess. Bess stayed awake for almost two days and even got out of her room and went down to the nurse's station. We never got the feeling to go visit Bess in the hospital again. She passed on the second day, but she had time to see everyone she was supposed to see one last time.

A few months later, when I was trimming the hooves of Ned's horses, he came over to me and told me he had thought I was nuts until Sharon told him abut the blue dress and the swing-dancing. He said there was no way I could have known about that. About six months after Bess had passed, Sharon called me. They were missing Bess's wedding ring and thought it might have been stolen. She asked me to pray and ask Bess where it was. I did, and Bess told me to look up high in the chandelier, where you wouldn't normally look. We went over to their house and it was like a treasure hunt, but the ring was not located. A couple more weeks passed and Sharon called. Sure enough they had found the ring. It was in a safe deposit box they had completely forgotten about, which was up high in a bank in Chandler (which sounds very similar to chandelier). I have done many readings where I'm shown one thing that could be interpreted many different ways. It's as if the ones in heaven are looking in my rolodex of life experiences and find something as similar as possible to help me to understand the message.

Approximately a year after Bess's passing, Rose came back into Ned's life. Rose and her husband used to double date with Ned and Bess as teenagers. When they had children, they used to go on family outings together. Rose's husband had passed away several years earlier. Shortly after that, Rose had brain cancer. The doctors said that she wouldn't be able to walk or talk, but she did. I guess she wasn't finished yet. Whenever Rose came around, Ned would get all silly and have a beautiful glow in his eye, like a kid again. It was very obvious that they were being put together. Shortly after that, Mo and I were out at a customer's house shoeing some horses when we got a call from Ned. He wanted to know if we would be witnesses at their wedding.

Of course we said yes. When I asked him when the wedding date was, Ned said "two–thirty." I asked him what day and he replied, "Today." I started laughing, because they were like kids running away to elope. So Ned married his lifelong friend Rose.

They had many good years together, considering Rose wasn't supposed to be able to take care of herself, much less Ned. Ned was completely dependent on Rose for everything from getting out of bed to eating and bathing. Rose gave happiness and love, which was what Ned needed most. Rose really seemed to keep Ned going. When Ned got sick and was put in hospice, Rose asked me to come and see him. When I entered the room, I could see that Ned was moving in and out of his body, almost like he wasn't sure if he wanted to pass or not. I could see him float around two feet above his body. Then sink back into his body. I could feel the peace.

The room felt very crowded, like the air was thick with angels. I told Rose I didn't think he would be here very long, and honestly for his sake,

I wished he would move on so he could be whole again. Ned was one of those people that if you looked into his eyes, you could see that he would not want to sit around very long. He had that look of a prankster; just waiting to mess with someone. On my way home, I saw a man in a wheelchair that looked like Ned. I knew it was him sending me a message that he had passed on. I had to smile to know that all of his worries were finally over. When I got home, I asked Maureen if we had gotten any calls and she said no. Five minutes later, Ned's grandson called to let us know that Ned had passed.

It's funny how we look at death as a tragedy and with such sadness. Even myself, communicating with them, I still feel sad; but on the spiritual side there is much happiness. No pain. No worries. You just turn into true love; pure love.

After I talked to Ned's grandson, I went into the bathroom to brush my teeth and I could not shut off the cold water. I twisted both knobs, but it was still running. I had to take off the hot water knob (which I wasn't even using in the first place), and tighten the nut before it finally stopped. Right when I was wondering how it had gotten loose, I saw Ned's face with a *"Gotcha!"* smile. At that same moment, Maureen yelled from the other room that she could feel Ned's presence. He is quite the prankster.

NEVER ALONE

I received a message from Jesus one night. He wanted me to call a friend immediately. This friend lived four hours away and had recently gotten a divorce. I called her and told her that the vision of her I saw was of her standing in the middle of her empty living room with no furniture, thinking that she was all alone. I told her that Jesus wanted me to tell her that she was not alone; that he would never leave her. She told me the room she was in was empty and that was exactly what she was thinking when the phone rang. I had never been to her house before, so accurately describing the room was Jesus' way of letting her know he was in the room with her.

GOD WATCHES OVER US ALL

I went to a new customer's house one day, Bill and Belle, to shoe two horses. We weren't there an hour when Bill told me he was a disabled veteran and he had been in an engine room when the engine blew up and killed his friend right in front of him. I knew right then I had been sent to him.

A few months later, I was lying in bed and I had a vision of two girls playing on the beach at the ocean. I had no idea who they were or who the vision was for until the next week. We went out to dinner with Bill and Belle and while we were eating, I got this overwhelming feeling to ask Belle questions about her self. I asked Belle about her family—where her dad lived, and how many kids in the family. It was just her and a sister, and her dad was from North Carolina. It hit me like a jolt, the message was for her. I guess at that point I jumped, like when you get a static electric shock, and I had a funny look on my face. It was like God just downloaded information to me all at once. They both asked me what happened.

I asked her when she had last talked to her dad. She said it had been years. I told her she needed to call him and tell him he needed to have his furnace checked, because he had a carbon monoxide or gas leak and I kept on getting the number four. She told me her dad was an atheist and would never believe that God was sending him a message. I repeatedly asked her to call him until she agreed to do it.

Two days later she called me to tell me that the day after she called her dad; he decided to have his furnace repairman out to check the furnace. The repairman found a crack in the heating chamber that was leaking carbon monoxide into his house. The repairman said it was a level four leak, the worst! Belle's dad started going to church shortly after that. I never made contact with him personally, but I'm sure he felt that if God went through that much trouble to reach out to him, the least he could do was reach back.

It's funny looking back at some of the people I've met and the readings I've done to see the outcome. Sometimes the message is to let people know that God is with them. Sometimes it's a loved one telling us they made the trip home to heaven safely so we don't have to wonder any more.

A woman called me on a referral one night. I was sitting next to the phone when it rang, but I felt like I should let the answering machine get it. The woman's son, James, had passed from a drug overdose in his senior year of high school, two weeks earlier. I wasn't sure if a reading was appropriate this soon. Up until this point, all the readings I had done were of people who had passed at least six months earlier. I prayed and asked God for guidance. He led her son James to me and I wrote down the information he wanted me to convey to his mother, Susan.

He told me that he was fine and she should not be angry with the person who gave him the drugs. He said that his hands were all better and he was driving. He passed his love to her and said for her not to worry, he was okay. I asked for something that would let her know it was him and that I wasn't just making it up. He told me to tell her not to start drinking again and he described his bedroom to me in detail, and that his bed had been moved. He also told her to go on the vacation she had just cancelled.

I called her back and related this to her and she started crying; so I asked her if she wanted me to stop. She said no, they were tears of joy, she was happy he was in heaven and to continue. His last message was to tell her that he was very happy now. By the way, she had just moved his bed. Susan also told me that James had problems with his hands from birth and could not get his driver's license because of it.

As I write this book, I think back to when I first started getting messages. I used to write them down. One of them was from Jesus: "You have begun a journey like no other; you need to pray and listen and I will give you the lessons you need to learn for this journey. First, you must always follow your heart. Be honest with yourself, whether or not you are accepted. You will know you reached out to them in the right way. I will lead you to them; you won't have to look very hard. Send peace and it will come back to you." I wonder sometimes where I am being led—where I will go. And I Realize I have become quite comfortable with my faith. I will go wherever God leads me.

FORGIVENESS

One day I was putting shoes on a horse. I had been shoeing Brenda's horse for around three years. I had the horse's foot in my hand, working away, and talking to Brenda at the same time. I really wasn't aware of what I was saying, God was speaking through me. I honestly couldn't tell you what I said to her, but I remember at the end I was choking on the words, thinking they were harsh words; something about a child being molested by her father.

I put the horse's hoof down and looked up at her. She had tears welling up in her eyes and I will never forget the deep feeling of sorrow I got—to this day it still upsets me to think about it. I knew that story I had told had been about her. The thought was very difficult, that someone could do that to this wonderful person, much less her own dad. I hugged Brenda.

I kept running through my head what had just happened; *How long she had been carrying this alone, unable to tell anyone?* We both cried and I told her that it was no wonder she had trouble getting close to God when she had been betrayed as a child by the person that she had complete faith and trust in.

I told her that God loved her and that to think how much she must mean to God to put all these things in action for three years, just to get to tell her how precious she was. That my being in her life for the past three years was how long it had taken her to trust me, so that I could deliver his message to her: A message of love and understanding, a message that she isn't alone and that God understands her, and a message of forgiveness. Brenda admitted that she had never told anyone. She had carried this immense weight alone. Her father had passed a few years earlier. I told Brenda she needed to talk to her husband, that she shouldn't carry this alone anymore. Forgiving someone who has passed is for us on earth to heal. When they come through from Heaven with their message they are whole again, all the human baggage is gone they come to me as pure love. Brenda is a very well-balanced wife, mother, and all-around person. She is a very bright light to all around her.

I got to a point where I wasn't second guessing anymore. I started asking God about different things that I would come across. I asked him one day about this little boy, about two years old, who was oxygen-deprived when born. I asked him why he would let this happen to this beautiful child. He told me that in this child's past life, he had been abused and had died of neglect. God told me to look at it spiritually. In this life, his parents had to do everything for him. He was very much loved and taken care of every minute of the day. It was fulfilling a contract, completing a circle.

As I write the pages of this book, I start to think of how God has reached out to everyone, including myself, and how he changed their lives once they were touched by his messages. Most of my readings end with the recipient feeling like a weight has been lifted, and in quite a few you can literally see the change. It is without a doubt proof that God, heaven, and angels are right here, right now, and all our relatives, friends, and pets are all around us. It's like stepping into the light for the first time.

ROSES FOR MARYANNE

We shopped at a local hardware store in our small town. We know quite a few of the people who work there. There is a woman who works there named Maryanne. One day while we were shopping I saw Maryanne and walked over to her. I told her that there was an older man in spirit form from Heaven standing next to her. He wanted me to relay a message to her. So I asked if I could call her that night to do a reading for her. She said it would be great, so I called her that evening. I had no idea what I was supposed to tell her.

I prayed before I called Maryanne, asking for God's guidance so that I would get the message for her clearly. I asked her who George was. She said it was her dad, who was still alive. I told Maryanne that I saw a vision of George Foreman, the boxer, and I wasn't sure what it meant. She laughed. They had just cooked dinner on their George Foreman grill, and she was at that moment washing it while we talked. I told her that her grandfather on her father's side said hello; he was referencing Mr. Green Jeans from the old Captain Kangaroo show. Maryanne laughed and asked who Captain Kangaroo was; I guess I was dating myself! Anyway, her grandfather liked to garden.

She asked her father the next day, and he said that he knew who Mr. Green Jeans was, and that his father used to always wear green coveralls. Her grandmother on her mother's side also came through; she wanted to let her know that she had not had a very good relationship with Maryanne's mother, Meg, but that she was working on it now. She was sending Meg yellow roses for friendship. Then she showed me the Pacific Coast, San Diego. Maryanne didn't know what that meant, so we moved on. Her grandparents came through to let her know they were there for her, supporting her.

The next morning, Maryanne had a knock at her door. When she answered it, it was her neighbor. He told her he had been visiting his son in San Diego and had seen these flowers and he felt like Maryanne should have them. They were a dozen yellow roses. Maryanne told me she started to cry, she was so shocked. She asked her neighbor if he knew me; she thought it must be a joke. He replied, "Who?" It was just a sign to prove to her that they're still here helping us and that we're not alone.

Maryanne had been betrayed in the past. She found it hard to trust people. This message was to help her heal, have faith and let her know everything was going to be alright.

In readings, I try to avoid the "relationship" questions. What I feel is if someone has to ask, "Is this the right person for me?" there must be something inside them saying "something is not right" or maybe the timing is wrong. One day, Maryanne asked me the "Is this the right person" question, and the answer I got was that she would find true love. I didn't think about it until I got off the phone with her. "You will find true love" meant no, whoever she was with was not the one. In this case, I believe God wanted her to know this, because like I said, I really try to avoid these questions.

Several months later, Maryanne said she met her "true love" and they got married. I felt that I should call Maryanne again. I told her that I had seen her with her husband and a little boy was between them holding their hands. I asked her if she was pregnant. She replied, "I don't know, am I? I don't think so." The next day, she called me back to tell me she was indeed pregnant. She gave birth to a beautiful baby boy. These repeated messages to me meant that Maryanne needed reassurance in God and that there are things going on all around us. Just look. God places signs around us. All you have to do is look for them.

SENDING US PEACE

My father passed a few years back. He stayed in his body long enough for my brother and me to make it to his side. It was difficult to see him that way, with tubes in him. They didn't think he would make it very much longer. When I walked into the room, he was surrounded by my family, with my mom standing to his right. They all looked very tired. I went to the left side of him and began to pray for peace for him. He previously had many strokes and had been bed–ridden for several years.

As I prayed, I heard him ask me telepathically to please remove the tubes. He didn't say it, but I knew he was asking us to let him pass. He seemed okay with it. My dad went to church and believed in God, but we had never really talked about it very much. We spent a little while sitting with him and then we all left the room so the nurses could remove the tubes.

After the nurses called us back into his room, it took only a few minutes for him to pass, but it seemed like it took forever. I didn't get any messages from him that night. I think because I was too distraught.

The next morning I went in the bathroom to brush my teeth and I was praying, asking my dad if heaven was everything that he had hoped it would be. I looked down and next to the sink was a newspaper, all folded back to be only about six inches wide. In big bold letters, it said, *"Apparently the Grass is Greener."* It was my Dad. I thanked him for the sign. I was the first one up that morning and no one had brought in the newspaper that morning. So how did it get there?

A few months later, my dad came to me and asked me to call my brother Artie to tell him that he was proud of him and that he (Artie) was a great husband and father. I asked my father for something to prove to Artie that it was him, and dad showed me a white trash bag being put into the trash compactor, which is supposed to only take black, thicker, bags. But Artie had run out of black bags, so on this day, he had used a white one. Artie laughed and thanked me for his message.

Dad later told me to call my sister, Donna, who was anxious to hear from him. He described the earrings she had on and directed her to the closet. I told Donna to look up on the shelf. Donna told me that there was nothing that meant anything to her... it was just stuff. Dad insisted that there was something there. The next day Donna looked in the closet that backs up to the one that Dad insisted in looking in and found a blanket of his. She just needed to know he was there. She now uses it when she watches television. She wraps herself up in it. Later that year, my sister moved to a new house and I was speaking to her when my Dad wanted me to tell her that the creaking in the upstairs hallway was him patrolling the hall. He thought it was pretty funny, as he always was a prankster, and he just wanted to be sure she knew that he hadn't left her.

When my oldest sister came out to visit, I told her that Dad was around. He told me to tell her that when her dog, Star, looks up at the wall and ceiling corner at her home, that Star was looking at him. When she was telling her daughters what I had told her, Star was staring at the corner I had described. Dad also described the clothes on the clothesline one time, again just to let her know he was still watching over her.

These messages are to let us know that heaven is all around us. The loss that we are feeling is physical not spiritual, urging us to see things through our spiritual eyes.

THE WEEK OF MARYS

One Sunday morning, Mother Mary came to me in a vision. I knew it was Mary right away. I am trying to find the words to describe her, but the more I try, the harder it is. The feeling is like she opened my soul, inviting me to come to her: extremely peaceful, very soft spoken, like a soft spring breeze. I tried to focus on her face, but it kept getting blurry, then into focus, then changing. I prayed to Jesus for help. I asked him if this was his mother; he then appeared and put his arm around her signifying, yes. Then her face changed and she was Mary Magdalene.

I didn't understand then what the message was, but now I refer to it as "The week of Marys." That morning, Maureen's Mom, whose name is Rita

Mary, called and was talking to her about Mary Rita, who is Mo's niece I believe that in getting this call God was saying, "Buckle your seatbelt, we are about to take off."

A woman named Wanda called me one evening. She delivered mail house to house and there was an elderly woman on her route named Mary, who had no living family. They had all passed on. She had no one to take care of her, so Wanda would take her shopping after work and checked on her every day. In the summer, Wanda would put Mary's air conditioner in the window for her when it got hot. This went on for a couple of years until Wanda got a promotion, so she was in an office all day.

Wanda had been in the office about a week when she got word that Mary had had a stroke and was found a couple of days later lying on the floor. Wanda felt awful. She felt like she should never have taken the promotion; that it never would have happened or that she could have helped Mary. I told her that there are some things we don't understand now, but there was a reason that it happened that way. And some day it will all make sense.

Wanda continued to visit Mary a couple of times a week in the nursing home and always made sure she was being taken care of. Mary made Wanda her Power of Attorney and Executrix, because she knew that Wanda was honest and she could trust her. Wanda had a very stressful job, so this was a big task for her to take on along with her own challenges. Mary was in the nursing home for three years.

Wanda called to tell me that Mary had passed that day. The Sunday of the week of Marys, she called and asked if I could please call her if Mary came to me. That Thursday morning I could feel Wanda's Mary around me. She wanted me to call Wanda. She told me that Wanda was having a bad day and could I please call her, so I did. Mary had left Wanda her house in her will and Wanda had a lot of guilt over that. She thought that people would think she only helped Mary for the money. Mary wanted me to tell her that she had helped a lot of people in her day, and when she got old the only people around her wanted to get paid for their services.

Wanda was the only one who had helped her out of the kindness of her heart. Wanda had rekindled Mary's faith in people, to see that there were still people like her that do things simply because it's the right thing to do. She told me that Wanda should have no guilt; she wanted Wanda to have the gift she had left for her. Mary then told me to tell Wanda to look out her back window, which she did, but she said she couldn't see anything because it was dark. Mary said to look for a shooting star. Wanda said that it was dark and there was too much cloud cover and she couldn't see anything.

The next night Wanda called to tell me her husband had taken the dogs out after I got off the phone with her and he saw a shooting star come right through the clouds and across the sky. What a beautiful sign to let them know everything's okay!

I know that this is one of God's lessons, to do things because it is the right thing to do. Not looking for any reward or personal gain. Originally when I spoke to Wanda about putting their story in this book she was apprehensive about it. Wanda was concerned about what people would think. Maybe they would think that she had only done it because Mary would leave everything to her. What I told Wanda was that it did not matter what everyone thought. All that mattered was she and Mary knew the truth that it was out of love. Wanda's proof came in the form of a shooting star.

Stephanie is a person I talked to frequently. She was originally unsure, thinking that she was all alone. Whenever I speak to Stephanie, I always get signs, like descriptions of the room she is in or things that happen in the days ahead.

Stephanie called me one day and left a message that she would like to speak to me. I had done a reading for her father a few months earlier. When I originally spoke with her, her life was upside down.

She knew of God and wanted to believe that he was in the here and now, but didn't believe that anyone could speak to him. A lot of people I do readings for think this; that God is not with them because they are ordinary people, insignificant. I told her that God was with her; that he didn't want her to be so unhappy, and that her uncle was also with her.

I immediately started to see things to prove that they were in the room with her, in the here and now. The first was that her roof was leaking. She started giggling and said that her roof *was* leaking. At this point, I could feel her curiosity building and that she was less nervous. Next, I was shown a medicine cabinet in the bathroom with a pocket watch hanging on it. She paused for a second and then with an excited voice said that she was in her bathroom looking into the mirror on the medicine cabinet and there was a pocket watch hanging on the side of it. Then I saw her picking glass out of her foot. She had dropped a picture just before I called and there was glass all over the floor. I then got an image of an African mask and the color orange. She had no clue about that, but the next morning on her way to work, she got on the subway and sat down across from a woman wearing an orange shirt with African masks on it. She told me that when this happened, she felt so overwhelmed that all she could think of was to get off the train. She got off at the next stop, even though it wasn't hers. I think that when I did the reading the night before it was surreal and when she saw that shirt she thought, *Oh my God, it's still happening.*

The next week she called me to tell me that a lot had happened. I told her not to misunderstand me, that this wasn't a magic trick. God was letting her know that he was still with her. Stephanie was in a place in life where she could see the signs to move on, but was afraid to take the first step. She was unhappy with where she was in her relationship. She was in a relationship that she wasn't sure of and was thinking of ending it. She was in a rut. Her boyfriend had an affair and was thinking about leaving her. I told her not to be sad about asking for a way out of something, whatever it was, and then being upset in the way it happens.

I told her that I too had a similar experience just recently. I had a friend that was like family. It was time for us to move on and we had let go of our friendship that week. She was also unhappy with where she lived and with her friends at the time. I told her that she was very sensitive to her surroundings and that an apartment building was not a good place for her. If the person downstairs was sad and the person upstairs was happy and the person to the left was frustrated and the one to the right was angry...well, with her being so sensitive, she would be picking up on all of that energy and wouldn't know how to feel. When I spoke to her, she was living in and apartment. I felt her energy. It was like it took everything she had to get through the day.

Stephanie called me and told me that she had moved out of her apartment and into a house with a couple of her friends. After she moved, she seemed very clear; she was making goals for herself and moving forward happily.

In the week of Marys, I also got a call from Stephanie, who called me every time she traveled to see if I got any messages for her. I talked to Stephanie about her trip to California and how she should move there; that she needed more sunshine and to be outdoors more. I also told her to watch for signs of doors opening for her, and that it was meant to be.

I asked her if she had a candle on a shelf in her living room. She said she did. Her uncle and grandfather had both passed, and her uncle was sharing this information to let her know that he was always around her and she was going to be alright. I then laughed and told her that I had been getting a bunch of Mary readings and I felt like she was going to bring up a Mary. She giggled and told me that the candle on her shelf was a Virgin Mary candle and the person she was going to stay with in California was named Mary.

The week of Marys I realized that God was making it easier for me, showing me one common thread "Mary." He was teaching me that all things have common threads; all you have to do is look for them. During the week of Marys God made it very easy for me to see this.

DINNER GUESTS

Some readings happen when you don't expect them. I guess you could say that you never know what is going to happen next or what is around the next corner. One thing is for sure is that God will lead and all you have to do is follow.

One evening we went to dinner at friends of ours' house, Bill and his wife Cathy. During dinner, Cathy's late husband, Dwayne, was standing in the doorway to the bedroom off the living room. He said he was from heaven and he had a message for Cathy. I was waiting, because I had that feeling of *"not yet."* About forty-five minutes passed when the door of the bedroom that he was standing in blew open from the window that was open behind it.

I told them that I was a messenger and that her late husband was there with a message for her. He sent his love and described many things to her to reassure her that it was him. While this was happening, I kept seeing a figure in the corner waiting his turn. Cathy was carrying some guilt over things that had happened in their relationship. I guess you could say he was mending fences, not for himself, but so Cathy could move on. Cathy and Dwayne had been separated when Dwayne passed. Cathy still had strong feelings about their relationship. I could see in Cathy's eyes that she was still mourning Dwayne. We never discussed why they got a divorce.

Once Dwayne got his message through, I focused on the person in the corner. I described this person to Cathy. I told her it was a man and he was dressed in black. When the message came to me, I didn't quite understand it until I said it out loud, "*Man in black.*" He said he was in the golden white light.

Well, there is only one person that comes to mind when I think, man in black…Johnny Cash. Cathy said she wasn't surprised. She said her late husband was a songwriter and he knew Johnny. He really didn't have a message for Cathy, but he did want me to pass one on to someone else. I did not yet know what it was or for who. Mo and I got home that night and turned on the television. It was on Country Music Television and the first thing on the screen was a full screen picture of Johnny Cash. Obviously, I was more than a little shocked. It was Johnny letting me know, "Yes, I need to send a message." I kept thinking to myself, *Which way should I go with this?*

A week or so passed when Marty Stuart came to mind. So I e-mailed him. It went something like this," I know this sounds crazy … "(I went on writing everything that Johnny wanted me to relay to Marty, a lot of which was personal and I don't believe should be put in this book.) Johnny spoke about a spear with feathers on it and said that he was proud of Marty. He also sent his love.

Marty's new album, "The Badlands," came out the next week. Marty dedicated it to the Lakota Indians. I believe that was what the spear and feathers were about.

I find it interesting how spirits find links through people here on earth to get their messages through. It is almost like they are saying "While you're listening, can you send a message for me too?" Just because a spirit comes in the color black it does not mean that they are bad. It is just a color nothing more. I think that if there were no horror films made God would find it a lot easier to get messages through to us. The horror films are only based on fear, fear of the unknown, and that all spirits are negative energies. Not all energies are negative. The ones from Heaven are here to help and guide us if we let them. When I pray to God and ask only for messages from him. I know without any doubt that God and only the spirits he sends to me from heaven are speaking to me when I pass on their message.

HOOTIE

One night, when I was lying in bed, a German shepherd came to me in a vision. He stood proud with his head high and chest out. I wasn't quite sure why he came. He just stood there looking at me with that, "Hello, I am here," look. The next night, he brought a man in army fatigues. They were standing side by side facing me. The next day, a friend came over to visit (I'm sure orchestrated by the shepherd and the man in the fatigues), and I told her about my vision. She told me I had to call her friend, Grace, who's German shepherd had just passed away and that she missed him terribly. His name was Hootie.

I called Grace that night. I told Grace about Hootie and that he had brought a man in fatigues with him. She said her father had been in the military. So I prayed and asked what the message for Grace was. Grace had a life–threatening illness, MRSA, and had been in a battle for her life. Grace is a very spiritual person who prays and always looks for guidance on which way to go. Grace's dad sent his love and told her not to give up.

Grace had been battling MRSA, a deadly staph infection. He told her she wasn't alone in her battle and he was with her every step of the way. He wanted me to tell her about the many adventures they had in life as a way of proving to her that he was there for her. He kept repeating for her not to give up; that this was not her time to pass. He spoke about when Grace was little, and the horse-shows, and how he called her his little champ.

A few months later, he came to me again and asked me to contact Grace to remind her of his presence and also to give his love to his wife, Laura. Their anniversary was coming up and she was missing him. While I was talking with Grace, he showed me the earrings he had given Laura as proof. Laura had worn the earrings to bed that night.

Grace's Aunt Missy came through also. She claimed that she had hidden one of Laura's shoes. I giggled and asked Grace if her Mom was missing a shoe. She was. Missy told me to tell them to look under the bed, *way* under the bed. Grace and her mom looked the next day and there it was, way under the bed. Grace told me that Laura used to play a joke on Missy when they were young and hide one of her shoes when she was sleeping.

Most of the time, when spirits come through to pass their message on, they still carry personality traits like Missy hiding Laura's shoe, always "the prankster". Other times they can be loud spoken or very quiet. Many times I can not stop smiling from their energy they are so happy to get their message through and to let us know how happy they are. These traits are a way of identifying them so I can describe them to their loved ones here on earth to let them know that it is them.

How I describe doing readings is like this: it is like walking out on to a stage in front of a crowd of people with this huge bright light on you and not knowing what you are supposed to say. Everything is quiet; you can hear a pin drop. Then God hands you a script and guides you through it.

GOD'S CONDUIT

A friend's name came up a few times one day. I hadn't spoken to her for about five years, so I figured something must be going on with her, so I called her. She laughed because she had been thinking of us too. Her name was Darlene and it was great talking to her and catching up. When I first met Darlene, she had her horse boarded at her fiancé's mom's farm. I had spoken to another horse there, and Darlene wanted me to talk to her horse. She asked me about the horse she had purchased and named Widow. It was pretty wild and didn't care for people. When Darlene purchased Widow, she had a big gash on her chest. Darlene had the vet out and when he tried to sedate Widow, the horse bit him and struck out at him with her front hoof.

You couldn't go into the stall with her because she would chase you out.

Darlene and this horse seemed to have a connection. So she asked me if I was getting anything spiritually. I had never seen this horse, but I started seeing a battle. Darlene and Widow were both in armor. I could feel an adrenaline rush and a forward charging motion. It was a fierce battle; Darlene's armor was covered with mud and debris. I saw a person with a sword swinging it at Widow, hitting her in the left knee and driving her to her knees. I asked Darlene if Widow had any scars on her left knee. With surprise, she answered that there was. Then I saw another person in the battle spear Widow in the right hip. Again, I asked if she had a scar on her right hip. Again she answered yes, that there was.

I told Darlene that Widow was back in her life because Widow had given her life for Darlene in a past life, and now it was Darlene's turn to heal Widow to complete the circle.

I have since seen Widow, and she is, in my experience, a very balanced horse. Darlene has done a great job healing Widow. She has taken Widow everywhere with her and has ridden her in many competitions. Darlene's five year-old daughter rides Widow all the time.

Darlene came back into our life for many reasons; one reason was for widow. Another reason is that Darlene travels quite a lot and meets many people. She is what I call a conduit. Darlene's life is very similar to ours, in her travels she finds people who have a message waiting for them and she either brings them right to our door or has them contact me.

Timing is everything in readings. The best way I can explain it is that when a person is open and ready to receive their message, we will meet them; not too soon and not too late. God has perfect timing, *divine timing*. I have done many readings for people that Darlene felt we could help.

Laura called me one evening. Darlene (the conduit) had given Laura my number. She was really worried about her twin sister Danielle, whose horse had recently passed. Danielle was still pretty upset. The first vision I saw was of a woman with a horse. The woman told me that she was there when the horse crossed over. Laura told me that her mother Sue had passed. Sue showed me herself taking big breaths, in and out. Laura said her mother had passed from serious lung problems.

Sue wanted to tell Laura not to worry, that she was there to greet Danielle's horse when he passed. Sue also said grandma was there with her. Grandma was showing me her bare feet. Laura laughed and said Grandma (Sadie) never wore shoes. Sadie said that she also had Evelyn with her. Sadie was standing on her front porch (with no shoes on) and swinging her arms like she was on "The Price is Right" opening door number two, swinging her arms to the left. Laura told me that Grandma's friend (Evelyn) in the house next door (to the left) had passed.

Sadie showed me herself and Evelyn playing cards. Laura said they had played cards all the time. Sadie wanted to tell Laura that it was okay, that Laura was not supposed to be there. Laura started to cry when I told her that. She had been living with her Grandmother and had gone to Las Vegas for three days when her Grandmother passed. Laura had been carrying a lot of guilt, feeling like she should have been there.

I think we all believe that if you die without anyone with you, that you die alone. This isn't true. We are never alone. Just like her sister's horse, there is always a greeting party. I wish I could make special glasses that would allow you to see all the help God has placed all around us. I told Laura that she was exactly where she was supposed to be. Grandma Sadie said it was supposed to happen that way, because she didn't want Laura to find her like that. Sadie said, *"Remember me in the good times."*

The very next day, I was at a customer's named Sue, trimming horses. I had been trimming Sue's horses for several months. The first time I trimmed her horses, we went into the house to get paid and I could feel a presence. I knew it was her grandmother. She was wispy, moving through the house very peacefully, enjoying the freedom of being in spirit form. She wanted me to tell Sue that she had done a great job healing in the past year, putting her pain behind her and moving forward.

Sue confided that she had just told her mother in the past year that she had been molested as a child. Sue said that she had been very close to her grandmother and missed her very much. I told her that the first time I met her, I could feel her grandmother around her, especially in the kitchen. Grandma then showed me her feet. I giggled because her grandmother was like Laura's, no shoes! Sue said she used to give her grandmother pedicures. I thought it was great that her grandmother had come through to acknowledge the personal growth that Sue had achieved.

I have found that God reaches out to all of us. It's about listening and being ready to hear what he has to say. At times, I think people are afraid to hear what he has to say. They think he's going to tell them something they don't want to hear. Sometimes that is true. But if you don't already have *"no"* for an answer, and truly listen to his whole message, you will see it's to help you. Maybe you aren't in the right place; maybe it's the wrong job, wrong house, and wrong surroundings. Most of this we may already know, but the task of changing can seem so overwhelming. It's just easier to stay stuck.

One thing that speaks louder than God is fear. Don't be afraid of change. If you let the fear go, and relax, that is when you hear God's voice.

Sometimes when God reaches out, it is through a total stranger, saying something to you that was just what you needed to hear right at that moment. He reaches out to technical people in a technical way. He may reach out to a deaf person with music or to a blind person with a beautiful vision. But if a person is ready and listening, he is standing right in front of us, waiting to guide us.

SIGNS ALL AROUND US

I was talking to my friend Jaye on the phone one evening, one of those catch-up calls. I told her that her mom was around her and wanted to let her know that she was here to support her. Jaye's mom's name is Starlette. Starlette told me that she was moving things around and that it was to help Jaye to tune in to what was going on around her. Starlette showed me a rake first. Jaye laughed, she always kept the rake in one spot; but the other day when she went to get it, she could not find it anywhere. When she did find the rake, she knew it was not where she had left it.

Starlette went on to tell me that she had been there when Jaye tripped the other day. Starlette said that she had tripped her. She said that she was trying to wake her up, to get her attention, to let her know that she was there. Jaye said that she did trip and almost knocked herself out on a pole. She had a big lump on her head. When she looked to see what she tripped on, there was nothing there.

Next, Starlette showed me a cooking timer, the kind that the bell goes off when the time is up. It was sitting on top of a microwave. I told Jaye that it didn't make any sense, because microwaves shut off when they're done. I knew that it meant something else. Then I heard the bell go off. I told Jaye this. We both laughed because neither one of us knew what it meant.

Throughout the reading I kept hearing a bell. Again I asked if this meant anything to Jaye. Jaye said it did not mean anything to her personally but she said that she had a friend named Sasha with a daughter named Belle. When Jaye said this, I immediately got a vision of a dog with glasses on. We both laughed. Jaye said that Sasha's daughter was three years old and her name is Belle and that she wore glasses. Jaye told me that Sasha had a hard time keeping glasses on Belle because Belle would take them off and try to step on them. I was a little confused at this time about the whole dog with glasses vision so we moved on to the next message. Then Starlette introduced me to an older woman. She was standing looking at her fingers like she was holding something. The feeling I received was that she had gone inward mentally, not responding to anyone.

I asked Jaye if Sasha's grandmother had passed from Alzheimer's. Jaye said she was not sure about Sasha's grandmother. Jaye asked me what she should do about this. I told her if she wanted to, she could talk to Sasha and ask her if she would like to talk to me about what our conversation was about.

Two days later, Sasha called to talk to me. She said she had spoken to Jaye. She told me she had a grandmother who had Alzheimer's disease who had passed. I told Sasha that a lot of readings I do refer to other readings. I also said to her that I was told to tell her about another reading because they were very similar.

I told her about a reading that I did for a woman in my living room. I told this woman, Pat, that her mother sends her love. Pat then asked me what her mom's name was. I told Pat that I don't usually ask for names, because names are for us. In heaven, you just know who it is. So I told Pat that I am seeing my mom's face and I am being told that it is really close to her name. I told her my mom's name was Edie. Pat immediately said, "Hi, Mom." She said her mom's name was Ada. When I told Sasha about this reading, she replied that her Grandmother's name was Edie.

Then I went on to say that my mom lived in Woburn, and that she owned a three family house, and that some members of my family rent the other two apartments from her. Sasha said that her grandmother also lived in Woburn and owned a three family house, and she also rented to family. When I told Sasha where, she said that was the same neighborhood that her grandmother lived in, in fact, my mom shops where Sasha's grandmother used to work. Talk about a small world. I believe that this was God's way of letting Sasha know that we are all connected, that we have a common thread. Also Sasha needed to know that she was not alone. That she shared a common thread with me.

I told Sasha that her grandma was trying to get her to move forward. Grandma Edie said that Sasha was frozen in fear; fear of moving forward in many different ways. And all she had to do was to take one step and that she would help.

I then told her that her sister Nancy was here. Nancy was saying that she was still here with Sasha and had never left. Nancy showed me herself sitting next to Sasha with her arm around her, and her head on Sasha's shoulder. While I was talking to Sasha, her daughter Belle was pretending she was a dog and was barking at her while she was on the phone with me (the dog with glasses on). Nancy also told me that Sasha had a ring of hers. Sasha said that she actually had two. Nancy told me that they were in Sasha's jewelry box on the right side of the dresser.

Nancy also told me that the tree that was planted in memory of her had died and she thought that was funny. Sasha didn't know what this meant. Nancy then showed me herself throwing a couple of ice cubes into her mom's lap, whose name is Ann. Again Sasha didn't know what this meant.

And then Nancy showed me a vision of her with a boy in front of her. He was wearing a jersey with the number four on it. Sasha told me that Nancy had lost a child, and the anniversary of his passing was in four days. Nancy went on to tell me that she was hiding the forks of her other sister, whose name is Tina. I believe that this was Nancy's way to get me connected with Tina and that she had a message for her. At that point, Sasha asked if it would be okay to give Tina my phone number. I said, "Of course it was."

I started to hear pots and pans clanking. Nancy and Edie said they were going to make them clank, so Sasha would know they were there. I then told Sasha that I was seeing a vision of her daughter's bedroom. In the upper left corner of the room, I saw a bright light. The vision was a fairy. Grandma said that was her. That was how she came to Belle.

Above the foot of the bed, I saw an angel. She was beautiful. She was animated with light colored hair, a blue dress, and wings. I then saw a picture of a man dancing. It was in black and white. I told Sasha about this. I then said that his name was something like Ernest Borgnine, the actor. Sasha told me that her father's name was Ernest and that he had passed. I said that they just wanted Sasha to know that they were watching over Belle.

Sasha asked me if she could contact me about the things in the readings that didn't make sense after they became clear to her. Five days later, Sasha contacted me and told me that the school that Nancy had worked at had planted a tree for her and it had died. They had planted a new one. Sasha also told me that on the anniversary of Nancy's son's passing, her mom, Ann, was on the way to the cemetery and stopped at a Sonic (a fast food restaurant) to grab a bite to eat. On the way to the cemetery, the bottom of the soda cup fell off, dumping all the ice into her lap. I guess we know what Nancy meant by the ice cubes.

At this point, Sasha handed the phone to her mom. Nancy wanted me to tell her that the ice was to shock her back to life and that Ann was not living life, she was just passing through it. Nancy wanted her mom to be happy again. Nancy sent her love to her mom and for more proof that she was there in the car with her, Nancy started showing me a peppermint candy cane in Ann's glove box.

I asked Ann if she had peppermint candy in the glove box. Ann said yes. The restaurant where she had gotten the soda gives peppermint candy with the meal. She had put it in the glove box.

My next conversation was with Tina who was Sasha's younger sister. Tina was very close to Nancy and missed her very much. Tina told me that she could talk to Nancy about anything and missed their conversations. I asked Tina if she was missing forks in the house. She replied, yes. I told her that this was Nancy's way of kidding around with her and to let her know that she was still there with her. I told her that her sister Nancy sends her love, and will always be with her.

GOD'S TOY BOX

My friend Kim called one day and asked if I could please call her back. She sounded very serious. I prayed for guidance, Kim's mom Laura came to me in spirit form and showed herself next to an archway of pastel flowers. Laura was motioning with her arms to pass through.

This was the first time I had ever seen anyone do this. I knew exactly what she meant. Laura was telling me that Kim was going to pass soon. I started to see if I could get any feeling of illness, but I didn't get anything. I said a prayer for Kim for peace. I called Kim right away. I asked her what was going on, and within ten minutes of talking she had a melt down. Kim was at the end of her rope. She was in relationship, financial, physical, and mental distress. She wanted to have children and be a mom. She wanted not to have so many financial worries. She wanted to have someone that would help her through all of her problems. But most of all, she wanted to be loved and cared for.

She told me she had no one and felt all alone. She told me she was going to take her own life. I've known Kim for at least twelve years; she is a very emotionally stable person. To hear her talk like that really surprised me.

I reminded Kim about a reading I had done for her several years earlier. It was in black and white. Kim was in an old car driving down the highway. She was very upset and crying, and then she turned into oncoming traffic and took her own life. I said that she was right back in the same place again this lifetime. We both knew that she had been given a chance to work through her problems in order to break the cycle and move forward.

I told her that God did not want her to be so unhappy, and that God certainly did not want her to hurt herself. I told her that she had made some decisions that she had to fix and all she had to do is ask for guidance and be willing to make changes. We talked for a few hours. I told her that she was a great, loving, caring person that deserves better, and that's what it's all about. Asking for help is not going to work if you don't feel worthy enough to deserve it. I then asked her if she ever heard of the book *The Secret*. I told her it was about getting back what you put out into the universe.

I call it God's toy box. I said that God's toy box has everything in it that she could ever want to make her happy and to feel worthy to receive it. I then said that she should do some affirmations. I told her that she should look in the mirror and say that she is worthy of true love, worthy of peace, and worthy of true happiness. I said that she needed to send out a different vibe than she had been sending. She needed to be open and ready to receive it.

I told Kim the more squeamish she felt about doing her affirmations, the more she needed to do them. That squeamish feeling translates to, *I really don't deserve this*. When I got off the phone with Kim, I continued to pray for her. I had hoped that she had changed her mind. The next day, I had her on my mind all day. Every time she would come to mind, I would pray for peace for her. The next evening, I called her to see how she was doing. She thanked me and said she felt much better. I told her that I loved her and to call me anytime.

Four months later, Kim called me and said that she did buy *"The Secret"* and loved it, and that it really helped. Kim said that the reading I had done for her had changed her mind. I was very deeply touched by her words. I have had people tell me that they were unhappy and that it would be easier if they were dead; but they were just words and they had never planned on going through with it.

ANGELS AMONG US

I have a friend named Maria who had suffered from cancer for years. She was a very loving, quiet person. I would visit her periodically, pray for her, and tell her everything was going to be all right. She thought that she had done some things in her life that were really bad and that she didn't think that she was worthy. I told her what I tell all people: God loves her and that the moment one asks for forgiveness and really wants it, he forgives immediately.

Unfortunately, we think that we have to carry with us everything we ever did wrong, like a backpack. When a person is born, it is empty, but as we move through life, we just keep on adding to it until we pass on. God does not want us to carry this burden. Isn't that one of the reasons why he sent Jesus to us? God sent Jesus to let us know that he does forgive. When your child does something wrong and you let him know it, do you punish him forever or do you forgive him and move on?

I would try to go and see Maria whenever I felt that we needed to talk. I remember trying to go see her for several weeks, but no matter what my plans were, the visit would never happen. One day, all my horseshoeing customers cancelled and I knew it was my door opening for a visit. When Maria opened the door, she was wearing a baseball cap to hide her lack of hair from chemotherapy. She only opened the door around six inches and peeked out. She looked so surprised to see me. Her eyes became wide and happy and she welcomed me with a huge smile. I walked in and sat down and we started talking. She told me that she was going in for more tests the next day and that she was scared. She said that she had been praying for me to visit. That's when I realized why I couldn't get there earlier. It wouldn't have helped as much. She needed me at that moment, not weeks earlier.

Maria ultimately passed on. She was a great mother, wife, friend, and teacher. She taught me that you must go on. I do believe that the eyes are windows to the soul. When I looked into Maria's eyes, she had a beautiful soul. I'm sorry for her family's loss, but she sure deserved to go home to heaven.

My friend Sandy passed from cancer. Before she passed, she came to visit Maureen and I. Sandy came to see if we could get any information from her angels. The feeling I got was that if she had the surgery that was supposed to save her life, there would be many complications.

It really scared me to give anyone advice on whether or not to have high risk surgery for a life-threatening illness. At first, I really shied away from any of her questions. I really did not want to say to just let the cancer take your life. I've seen miracles and I do believe they happen. I also believe that God can heal through doctors.

I told Sandy that I got a vision of her sitting at our kitchen table having breakfast with the sun shining in on her. Sandy told me that vision was what kept her going the weeks after her surgery. Of course, her family was all there for her. Sandy passed ten weeks after her surgery. Two days later, I went out to my truck to warm it up and when I started it, the CD player went on. It went to the twelfth song *(Spirit in the Sky,* by Norman Greenbaum). At first, I was surprised at it going to the twelfth song, but then I got a vision of Sandy's face with a great big smile. She was dancing all around with a tambourine. This was her way of showing me that she was happy and healthy and had found her peace. The CD was given to me by my son and I never listened to the whole CD. I didn't even know that song was on it until that day.

When I thought about the vision I had for Sandy, I did not understand why she never made it up to our house to have that breakfast. One morning, I got up and made breakfast. When I looked over at the kitchen table the morning sun was shining in on it. It had golden rays shining on the table, and one chair, the one I saw in the vision; and I knew that she did make it to that breakfast, in the golden white light of heaven. What a peaceful, loving, kind, spiritual person.

Life is so busy. We all try to keep busy and keep moving forward. Sometimes we forget to feel God's rhythm. Only God knows when the timing is right.

I have been praying for a change in my life. But like most people, I have been resisting my answer. God is trying to answer my prayer, so today I have decided to continue to write and stop resisting, and write more readings in his book. I have been realizing how much the readings through God have changed my life for the better. He has told me that he was happy that I was back. How patient he is. Thank you.

I have a hard time not getting emotional when God speaks to me.

A very humbling experience it is.

Sitting here looking at the candle that I light for Jesus, I get a vision of myself putting my hands around the top of the candle and it lights by itself. Then God tells me that I did that, but I can't tell anyone.

The candle was lit by God, and no one else saw it light. It doesn't mean it didn't happen. You know it and God knows it. Does it really matter if anyone else knows? It's between you and God, and its called *Faith*.

I keep feeling for timing: timing to write this book; timing for readings; timing as to when I should listen up, when something is about to happen. The readings I have done have been very educational to me spiritually. I have learned something from every reading. Sometimes, I wonder if it's like the horse that brings the owner to us, for the messages; are all of these readings for me to learn from, bringing me to God like a God college course on spiritual growth?

The first eight and a half years of readings, I did not try to remember what the readings were about, because it was for the recipient, not me. Another reason is not to keep score, not to feed ego, because it's not about how many, it's about doing it right, and doing everything you are supposed to for every reading. When I started to compile messages for this book, I was really surprised at how many there were.

I now know where my resistance comes from. It comes from the emotions from every reading. Some were very difficult to do. To feel a portion of what the recipient is feeling, and to look into their eyes is very difficult. What keeps me going is that God has led them into my life, to help them, to ease their pain.

God does not want us to be unhappy. He loves us very much, more than we can possibly understand. It is a very "drop to your knees" humbling feeling to know this.

NO BOUNDARIES

I know a woman named Jill. She is a mobile veterinarian for small animals. She called one day and was very upset. She just had to put her dog Sophie to sleep. Sophie had a good long life with Jill. Jill was very upset about letting her go. As we talked on the phone, I started to see the color pink. Jill said that Sophie was wrapped up in her favorite blanket next to her, and it was pink.

Sophie relayed to me that she was going to stay with Jill in spirit form. Sophie showed me that while Jill was sitting at her desk, Sophie was sitting next to Jill, to her right, looking up at her. Jill told me that she was in her office at home at her desk.

I have seen pets stay around their owners for years. I always tell people that their animals do go to heaven, and that heaven is all around us. I wish we could wear glasses that would let everyone see them. We wouldn't feel so alone when we lose someone.

We had a friend, Tina, come to our home one day. We had had the spiritual talk with her a week or so earlier. She came over to talk to us about her friend, Allie. Allie had a three-year-old daughter, Jackie, who had many seizures from a brain stem tumor. Tina wanted to know, "If there was a God, why he would do this to a three-year-old? What kind of sins could Jackie have possibly done to deserve that?" I told Tina that I don't question God's will, but if he would like to tell me, then I would let her know.

That night, when I was praying, God came to me and told me that when this three-year-old's body was forming, there were several souls around it. He said that one of the things in this body's contract is at three years old, there would be these problems and that they were to bring Jackie's mom, Allie, closer to him. When this happens, the surgery for the tumor would take place on Saturday. I relayed this message to Tina.

This was on Wednesday. You could feel her wanting to believe, but there was a lot of hesitation. Tina called on Thursday to tell me that she had spoken to Allie, but hadn't told her what we had talked about. Allie was very upset because Jackie was having a lot of seizures and the hospital could not fit her in for surgery until Monday. Well, Tina at that point was unsure, to say the least, if I was making it all up.

Friday, Tina called to inform me that Allie had called her and said that she was in church praying with a priest when she received a call from the hospital telling her that they just got an opening on Saturday for Jackie's surgery. Well, Tina was a little more open to the thought of *Maybe there really is a God*. I'm not saying that our loved ones pay the price for our lessons. It is about one of the many things we are supposed to accomplish in our lives.

The message I get through the readings I have done is that everything in our lives is not predestined. But I do believe there are several things we have to do in our lives that are carved in stone, and everything in between is *"freewill."* That's the part where our lives seem to coast. When you hit one of those "carved in stone" times is when everything seems to be going really fast with high energy, like you're not in control.

Maureen and I used to teach classes on how to get in touch with God, Guardian angels, and animals at our house. The group would range from three to eight people. Basically, it was about quieting your thoughts enough to hear God. I think these days, things happen so fast, everyone feels like they need to stay ahead of the wave or get left behind, which is funny, because when you're at the ocean and you see a wave rolling in, the water is always calm behind it. I am surprised at how many people have such difficulty in quieting themselves.

We had a meeting one night, and there was a new lady who came with her friend. I told them that our meeting was about God and that sometimes he comes to us through other people, the same way our loved ones come to us from heaven. We told them if something popped into their heads and it didn't make any sense, it could be a message for someone in the group. So we encouraged everyone to say whatever came to mind, no matter how silly it may have sounded.

We were about twenty minutes into the meeting when I got a vision of a lemon meringue pie. So I asked if this meant anything to anyone. We all giggled and everyone said no. So we went on with the meeting. Fifteen minutes went by and I got the same vision again, so I asked again and I got the same reply, no.

The woman sitting to the left of me, Candy, started telling the new woman, Beth, that she had someone here for her, but she was having trouble focusing on whether it was a woman or a man. Around two seconds after Candy said that, it hit me like a ton of bricks, like an information download. I said that it was a man and his name was

Randy. Beth almost fell off the couch. This was her first meeting and she had never met us before. This really caught her off guard. She said her late husband's name was Randy. I told her Randy was sending apologies. He said that he had been abusive in life and did not treat Beth the way she should have been treated. He sent apology after apology asking for her forgiveness and asking her to move on. He did not want her to remember him like that. He also did not want her to carry that pain anymore. I then asked Beth what kind of desserts Randy used to eat. She said he really didn't like any sweets except lemon meringue pie. I guess it wasn't so silly after all.

This was one of my lessons in humility. Sometimes the message may seem very strange and I know people are going to laugh. But if I hold it in and do not open my mouth Beth would not have received her message. I believe every message is important no matter how large or small it may seem to me.

LOVE AGAIN

I was at a shoeing customer one day. I used to trim Cindy's horses hooves every eight weeks. I knew she was a widow, but we never talked about her husband's passing. I had just finished trimming her horses and I got the *"tell her"* vibe, so I began telling her how I could hear and see people who have passed. She took it pretty well. I guess it was her time. I asked Cindy if she wanted me to do a reading for her. She replied, yes. I told her that her late husband, Paul, was next to her. He told me that he wanted her to move on. He said he wanted her to live and love and that it was okay to love again.

Cindy said she had been seeing a guy and that she was afraid of getting close to him, because she felt like she was betraying Paul. He insisted that she love again and that he would be in heaven when she passed. I then got a vision of tropical flowers and a headstone, and the feeling of Hawaii. I asked Cindy if Paul was buried in Hawaii. She replied, no. So I asked her again. She replied, no, again. Then Paul showed me Cindy standing on the rocks tossing dust into the ocean. Cindy said she did that with his ashes in Hawaii. We both giggled when I said, "So he's buried in Hawaii."

CELEBRATE LIFE

I had a couple, Bob and Tanya, over at our house one weekend. We were sitting down talking about people who have passed and how I receive messages from them. I used Tanya for an example. I said that I focus on that person's energy and then I zoom back and feel the energies around them. I told Tanya that she had a lot of energies around her. Then one stepped forward and said he was Tanya's cousin, Simon. I told Tanya that her cousin felt like a man, but was very soft–spoken like a woman, opposed to being loud and boisterous.

He told me that his birthday was October fifteenth. Tanya and I argued about the date. She said it was the twelfth. Simon repeatedly told me it was the fifteenth. Simon said that his mom (Virginia) grew yellow roses in memory of him. He showed me cliffs at the ocean. He also described several things in his mom's house. I remember that the feeling of Virginia's house was very still, like everything had stopped living. One of the things he described was a glass cabinet in the corner of the room. It was round in front. It had a picture of Simon in it. Simon said that it had been moved recently.

Simon wanted his mom to know he was in heaven. He did not carry his pain anymore. He had found happiness. He also said he wanted his mom to celebrate his life and not to mourn his death. (Virginia used to go to Simon's grave every birthday.) Simon's mom lives in Portugal; with the time difference, Tanya had to wait till the next day to call her and give her the message.

That next afternoon, Tanya came up to me at the local swap meet and gave me a great big hug. She said her aunt sent it. Tanya's Aunt Virginia informed Tanya that she did grow yellow roses in Simon's memory and the description of the room was correct. Virginia had taken out and cleaned Simon's picture the day Simon said that it had been moved (the day of Tanya's reading). She also did live near some cliffs by the ocean. The message that he was in heaven was very important to Virginia, because Simon took his own life. Virginia believed that her son was burning in hell. I can't imagine how much pain she must have been in believing that. On Simon's next birthday, October fifteenth, (which was a week after Virginia received her message from Simon) Virginia cut some of the yellow roses she had grown for him, brought them down to the ocean, threw them in, and celebrated his life knowing that her son was in heaven.

This message is complicated, because I tell everyone that taking your life is not the way out. I do believe in reincarnation and that if you take your life, you will be back to work through it again. I tell people in my messages that God is our heavenly Father and that we are his children. He loves us more than we will ever know. I also say that if we had a child that did something wrong, we wouldn't torture them for eternity. We would want them to learn from their mistakes and move forward. I also believe that suicides are lessons for us all to reflect on our own lives and to think about how our lives aren't really that bad, and what could have pushed someone that far not to want to come back. Simon was never alone in his struggle.

SHOWING FAITH

A friend called me one morning. Rhonda told me her horse had a neurological problem. He would be very unstable when he walked. I asked whether we should go and pray for her horse, and see if we could heal him. God answered "Yes." I called Rhonda back and told her I was canceling the next day's work and we would be there. She lived one hundred and eighty miles away. A couple of hours after I told Rhonda we would come, I started to get the feeling that we weren't going for the horse. I started to question whether we should go, but I kept thinking *I know I received my message right: "Go"; and I didn't get a maybe.*

So that next morning, we went. When we pulled up, there was a woman there who had boarded three horses with Rhonda. Her name was Beverly and her daughter's name was Faith. We did our healing on Rhonda's horse and talked to one other horse. Rhonda privately asked me if I was getting anything on Beverly; I turned to look at Beverly. She was standing in the aisle of the barn. I said yes, there is a man standing next to her in spirit. When I stepped out of the horse's stall into the aisle, Beverly asked me if I would talk to her horses. I told her I would, but I said that I would like to do a reading for her first. I explained how I did readings and that I only talk to heaven, nothing else, and she agreed. I immediately understood why we were told to make the trip. It was for Beverly.

I described this man to her. Beverly told me that I described her late husband Rick. Rick then repeatedly told me, "number five, number five." Beverly told me that they had five kids, and she was getting married in May, the fifth month. Rick relayed through me that he loved Beverly very much and that it was okay to move on and that he didn't want her to be alone.

Rick then showed me a dresser. He told me that there was something of his in the front right hand corner of the top drawer. Beverly told me that there were pictures there, along with his ashes. Rick then showed me an engagement ring. When I told Beverly this, she showed me her engagement ring. I told her, "not that one." Rick showed it to me repeatedly. I then told Beverly there was another ring. I told her that she must look at it frequently; by the way Rick was showing it to me. Beverly said she kept the engagement ring Rick had given her in the bathroom and looked at it every day. I think that by doing this, she was not letting herself move on. Her guilt of feeling like she was betraying Rick was holding her back. Rick wanted Beverly to love again and to pursue happiness.

I then asked Beverly if it was okay to talk to her daughter, Faith. Beverly said it would be fine. So I asked Faith if she understood what I was doing. She said yes. I told Faith that her dad was with her and that he loved her very much. Rick also said that he was very proud of her. Rick then showed me a vision of Faith's bedroom. Rick showed me Faith's bed and nightstand, and on the nightstand, he said that Faith had a picture of him. Rick told me that he was going to prove to Faith that he was still with her by moving that picture.

A couple of days later, Faith went home and when she went to her bedroom, Rick's picture had been moved. They were in a straight line. Faith had the three pictures in a semi circle. It is touching to know that Rick was still looking over Faith and reached out to prove to her that he is still in every moment her life. That was why God had us travel that day; to let Beverly know that he was still here, that Rick still loves her, and that everything was going to be all right.

REINCARNATION

During the first year of receiving messages, I was like a kid with a new toy. I had so many questions about everything. Sometimes, I felt like I was moving so fast that I looked like I was on one of those machines that the astronauts tested the G forces with.

One of those questions was about reincarnation. I would ask about people that I had in my life at that time. One of those people was Marcy. I asked God that if there was reincarnation, what was Marcy in a past life? Up until this point in my life, I thought that the whole idea was ridiculous.

God showed me Marcy standing at a bench. She had short black hair with her bangs cut straight across. There were herbs hanging up behind the bench. She was grinding up some in a hand held bowl in her left hand and some kind of a grinder in her right hand, at this point my vision froze. I didn't know that it was called a mortar and pestle at this time. So she was an herbalist. This didn't help me with my question of reincarnation, because there was no proof.

Three weeks later, I was at a Christmas party at a friend's house. Marcy was there. So I told her that I had used her as a guinea pig on my question of reincarnation. I described to her my vision. When I got to the part of the grinder, she said "a mortar and pestle, like the one I just bought." I started to laugh. I thought that they were playing a joke on me. I turned to my wife and asked her if she had told her about my vision. Maureen looked at me, laughed, and said no. That's when Marcy reached into her bag and pulled out her little mortar and pestle with the sales sticker still on it. Well, this had my attention. I was thinking, *what were the odds of that*. Then Marcy told me that she was an organic supplement distributor and a biochemist, which I didn't know.

Well, at this point, I became a believer, which led me to another set of questions, like, why? Why would someone want to leave heaven? Maybe you're not leaving at all, heaven is all around us. Maybe you just see things differently as a human, with all of our emotions and baggage; rather than a spirit, who is just love and understanding. I found that when a person is ready to hear the answer to their question, it doesn't take long for the reply.

One of the answers to my question was God's promise that when we pass on to Heaven and we look back at our lives we will understand why everything had to happen at that exact time. And it will make perfect sense. There will be no more questions, and you may think, *I did some really good things in my life. I helped a lot of people and changed a lot of lives. I would like to do that again, why not?* Or, *I would like to stay in heaven* (which is all around us, so you really are in the same place but different realms) *because I feel I would do my best work on this side, guiding people.*

Either way, you're still doing God's work: helping each other move forward. I'm not saying I know all the answers. I'm also not saying that I asked all the questions, but what I have found is I do get the answers when I need them, at the right time in my life. And being human, I still pause at the answer part, apprehensive of what it might be. Sometimes the pause is long, sometimes it is short. But either way, it's the right time when I receive it. Maybe not at what I would consider a good time, but I do believe it is in God's timing.

DIVINE TIMING

I see Laura frequently and I had done a reading for her the year before. A few weeks before I saw her, her brother-in-law, Bill, had passed away in a truck accident. When I talked with Laura, I told her how sorry I was for her sister Correy's loss. Correy had five children and no life insurance for Bill. During this time, I could see Bill in spirit form standing next to Laura, but I got the *"not yet"* feeling. So I told Laura if there was anything I could do for Correy, to let me know. I offered to take care of the horses' hooves for Correy, but they had already let the horses go. This was a sign to me that it was not time to get a message to her.

Six months later, I kept hearing the song "Cowgirls Don't Cry" by Brooke's and Dunn, at least seven times in one day. I had seen Laura early that afternoon and told her if Correy was ready for a reading, that I would be happy to either go to her house or pass her the message by phone. Laura was happy to tell her sister and she did call Correy that day.

When I got home that night, Correy had already left a message asking me to please call her. I called her that evening and told her I receive messages from heaven, like when you go on a trip and call to tell everyone that you made the trip all right. I asked her if she knew the song that I'd been hearing all day, and she began to cry. The song is actually about a father and daughter, but the message is about moving on through the bumps of life.

Correy's bump had been more like a mountain. Bill told me that he had been careless and he was sorry for the pain that he had brought Correy. He sent her his love and said he was with her still and that he was going to manifest a job for her that she would enjoy. Then he pointed to her ear, laughed, and said that she knew the joke. I was very curious at this point. I really wanted to know the joke, but I didn't want to intrude. Correy said that the first thing she thought of was that Bill dressed up as a pirate last Halloween and that he was a pretty funny guy. Bill told me to tell Correy to lean on her dad, that he would be there for her, and that she shouldn't go through this alone. Bill also told Correy that she wasn't losing her mind; everything was going to be all right.

I asked if she had any questions. She replied that she was still trying to hash through some of the things I had told her. I said that if she did have questions, she could call me anytime. The next morning, I was driving to a customer's house when I felt Bill with me. I asked him what part of that song he wanted to convey to Correy. He told me that I was like the phone company. This is the part of the song Bill wanted to convey. The lady in the song's father is passing and the phone is put next to his head so he can talk with his daughter. He tells his daughter:

"Cowgirls don't cry,
Ride, Baby, Ride.
Lessons in life show us all in time,
Too soon God will let you know why.
If you fall, get right back on.
The good Lord calls everyone home.
Cowgirl, don't cry."

GRANDMOTHER'S LOVE

One evening, I was talking to one of my customers on the phone. Her name is Natalie. She told me that her daughter, Samantha, was having some trouble. Samantha felt like she was different and just wanted things to go back to the way they were. She was diagnosed with type–one diabetes. Samantha was very athletic and was on the go all the time. She was in high school and really enjoyed sports. Since she was that active, she really needed to keep track of her insulin level, as if being a teenager wasn't rough enough.

Samantha got on the phone with me to see if I was getting anything on her. I told her that her grandmother on her Mom's side was with her and that she was showing me herself driving around on the passenger's side of Samantha's car. Peggy (grandma) said that Samantha was a great driver and she was very proud of her. Peggy also said that she was around her all the time. Peggy then directed me to the glove box in Samantha's car. Peggy said that there were pictures of her in there. Samantha said she didn't have any in there. Peggy insisted. Peggy then showed me a camera in the glove box. Again, Samantha said no. She said she only had a cell phone. I asked if it took pictures, and she said yes.

Peggy then showed me a picture of Samantha on some rocks by a stream. Peggy showed me a glimmer by Samantha's leg and said that was her. Samantha started to look through the pictures and found one where she was sitting on some rocks by a stream; it was taken on her sixteenth birthday. Yes, Grandma was there; right next to Samantha's leg, glimmering away like a shining star. I thought that it was so beautiful that Peggy went through all that to show Samantha that she was, and is, there for her.

I went to shoe two horses for a new customer named Darcie. When I started working on the first one, I got a feeling from a woman who wanted to send a message to Darcie. When I finished putting the shoes on the horses, I told Darcie that I passed messages to people from their loved ones who had passed on. I told her I had a message from either her mom or her mom's mother. She said her mom was still alive. I told her I was being shown an old sewing machine and something about the number two. She repeated the number two over and over.

Darcie said she had two of her grandmother's sewing machines. Her grandmother sent her love and showed me a birthday cake with two candles on it. I wasn't sure of the meaning of the two candles, but her grandmother repeated it over and over, two candles. Darcie's birthday was two weeks earlier and she had celebrated it with her mom. Her grandmother had passed twenty-two years ago when Darcie's son was two. Her grandmother had driven her to the hospital when Darcie had two broken arms, and her son was also born on the second. I guess that's what she meant by all the twos.

Her grandmother wanted to let her know that things were going to pick up at a faster pace for Darcie. She told Darcie to look for a small item on a shelf that would be moved; that she would know by the dust where the object was. Some of the readings I do, I never ask any questions, as much as I would like to ask them about the reading. I feel like if they want to talk about it they would bring it up.

God assures me that when we pass, we will know why everything happened in our lives and how it had to happen in that exact way at that exact time. Occasionally, God tells me why and I am blessed with his insight.

EPILOGUE

I was lying in bed one night thinking about this book, and how it all came together over the past years. How thankful I am to be chosen to be a messenger of God's; he reminded me of when I went out to feed our horses one afternoon. The sun was behind some clouds.

I was standing in the doorway of our barn when I heard a calling from heaven. It was a very peaceful, soft, *drawing–me–closer* feeling. I stepped around the corner of the barn so I could see the western sky; it was beautiful. The rays of the sun were gleaming through the clouds; beams of light shining down hundreds of them down on God's great earth. It was God and he told me that, "This is the best thing that you have ever done in your life." He touched my soul.

I woke up at ten o'clock one night; I was laying there in bed when God came to me and said that this book is a love letter to all who will read, all who are drawn to it. We will never know how vast his love is for us, no matter what we do or what we say, whether we believe in him or not. God is always there for us. God's love is so deep that we could not comprehend it. God's love is so understanding, that it's beyond our capability to understand. This book is not even the tip of the iceberg on how God loves us. God's everlasting love for us … What else can I say? I could go on all night trying to describe God's love, but words can't explain. All I can say to everyone reading this is to reach out. Reach back, God will be there. I have, and it's been an amazing eye–opening journey. Let God's love in. It will never end.

Look for the light; reach out; God is here.

All you have to do is *listen*.